I think the series is wonderful and beneficial for tourists to get information before visiting the city.

-Seckin Zumbul, Izmir Turkey

I am a world traveler who has read many trip guides but this one really made a difference for me. I would call it a heartfelt creation of a local guide expert instead of just a guide.

-Susy, Isla Holbox, Mexico

New to the area like me, this is a must have!

-Joe, Bloomington, USA

This is a good series that gets down to it when looking for things to do at your destination without having to read a novel for just a few ideas.

-Rachel, Monterey, USA

Good information to have to plan my trip to this destination.

-Pennie Farrell, Mexico

Great ideas for a port day.

-Mary Martin USA

i

Harrison Callaghan

Aptly titled, you won't just be a tourist after reading this book. You'll be greater than a tourist!

-Alan Warner, Grand Rapids, USA

Thank you for a fantastic book.

-Don, Philadelphia, USA

Even though I only have three days to spend in San Miguel in an upcoming visit, I will use the author's suggestions to guide some of my time there. An easy read - with chapters named to guide me in directions I want to go.

-Robert Catapano, USA

Great insights from a local perspective! Useful information and a very good value!

-Sarah, USA

This series provides an in-depth experience through the eyes of a local. Reading these series will help you to travel the city in with confidence and it'll make your journey a unique one.

-Andrew Teoh, Ipoh, Malaysia

GREATER THAN A TOURIST – BARCELONA, SPAIN

50 Travel Tips from a Local

Harrison Callaghan

Harrison Callaghan

Cover designed by: Ivana Stamenkovic
Cover Image: https://pixabay.com/en/panorama-the-cathedral-427997/

Greater Than a Tourist
Visit our website at www.GreaterThanaTourist.com

Lock Haven, PA
All rights reserved.
ISBN: 9781980946809

>TOURIST

50 TRAVEL TIPS FROM A LOCAL

Harrison Callaghan

BOOK DESCRIPTION

Are you excited about planning your next trip?

Do you want to try something new?

Would you like some guidance from a local?

If you answered yes to any of these questions, then this Greater Than a Tourist book is for you.

Greater than a Tourist Barcelona, Spain by Harrison Callaghan offers the inside scoop on Barcelona. Most travel books tell you how to travel like a tourist. Although there is nothing wrong with that, as part of the Greater Than a Tourist series, this book will give you travel tips from someone who has lived at your next travel destination.

In these pages, you will discover advice that will help you throughout your stay. This book will not tell you exact addresses or store hours but instead will give you excitement and knowledge from a local that you may not find in other smaller print travel books.

Travel like a local. Slow down, stay in one place, and get to know the people and the culture. By the time you finish this book, you will be eager and prepared to travel to your next destination.

Harrison Callaghan

TABLE OF CONTENTS

DEDICATION

This book is dedicated to my fiancé, Reece, my gorgeous new-born nephew, Leo and my puppy, Beau…

You hold my life together to make it as beautiful as the mosaics of Barcelona.

Harrison Callaghan

ABOUT THE AUTHOR

Harrison is a freelance writer and student who lives in Barcelona. He fell in love with the city when he was around ten years old, after seeing a picture of Gaudi's famous Sagrada Familia, and likening it to what he imagined the Emerald City of Oz would look like. Since the age of being able to travel by himself, he has made a yearly trip to this artistic city to pay it homage, until last year when he moved there as part of his language studies. He loves to read and write, he loves art and he loves good conversation; all things which Barcelona provides him with daily.

Harrison loves travelling in general, but he has always had a soft spot for Spain. In 2011, he walked the entire of 'The way of Saint James: The French Route', a near nine-hundred-kilometre trek across the north of Spain. After meeting his partner of five years soon after, they have talked frequently of moving to this iconic city, as it now feels like a second home; it was even where Harrison proposed.

Harrison Callaghan

HOW TO USE THIS BOOK

The Greater Than a Tourist book series was written by someone who has lived in an area for over three months. The goal of this book is to help travelers either dream or experience different locations by providing opinions from a local. The author has made suggestions based on their own experiences. Please do your own research before traveling to the area in case the suggested places are unavailable.

Harrison Callaghan

FROM THE PUBLISHER

Traveling can be one of the most important parts of a person's life. The anticipation and memories that you have are some of the best. As a publisher of the Greater Than a Tourist book series, as well as the popular 50 Things to Know book series, we strive to help you learn about new places, spark your imagination, and inspire you. Wherever you are and whatever you do I wish you safe, fun, and inspiring travel.

Lisa Rusczyk Ed. D.
CZYK Publishing

Harrison Callaghan

OUR STORY

Traveling is a passion of the "Greater than a Tourist" series creator. Lisa studied abroad in college, and for their honeymoon Lisa and her husband toured Europe. During her travels to Malta, an older man tried to give her some advice based on his own experience living on the island since he was a young boy. She was not sure if she should talk to the stranger but was interested in his advice. When traveling to some places she was wary to talk to locals because she was afraid that they weren't being genuine. Through her travels, Lisa learned how much locals had to share with tourists. Lisa created the "Greater Than a Tourist" book series to help connect people with locals. A topic that locals are very passionate about sharing.

Harrison Callaghan

WELCOME TO
> TOURIST

Harrison Callaghan

INTRODUCTION

*"Barcelona," Don Quixote
exclaimed, is a "fountain of
courtesy, shelter of strangers,
hospice to the poor, land of the
valiant, avenger of the offended,
reciprocator of firm friendship, a
city unique in its location and
beauty."*

Miguel de Cervantes Saavedra, Don Quixote, 1605

The best advice I could give to anyone looking to visit Barcelona is to go with an open mind, an eager heart…and an empty stomach. Spain, I feel, is one of the most underrated holiday destinations around. Brits like me choose to go to Spain for its cost-effectiveness for us, and then most of the time, we try to live as much like we are at home as possible. I cannot speak for the rest of the world of course, but from the tourist demographic I have seen, I can't help feeling it deserves a little more credit.

Harrison Callaghan

In relation to other developed countries in Europe, Spain sometimes seems a little behind; their last dictator only dying around forty years ago. Catalonia, a region in the North East, was poorly affected by the regime of Francisco Franco and the Catalonian identity was almost crushed. Barcelona, the capital of the Catalonian region of Spain carries with it a lot of painful history, which has fuelled a city of art, of music and of beauty and passion.

In this book, I will be giving you tips on how to appreciate Barcelona and Spain to its fullest, with tips for before and during your stay. I hope you enjoy discovering my Barcelona.

1. FALL IN LOVE BEFORE YOU GO

And no, I don't mean literally. If you know nothing of Spain and in particular, nothing about Barcelona, then I implore you to look, to read, to watch, to listen…

Reading any book set in Spain, historical or current will paint a picture of post-civil war struggle, which blossoms into an explosion of liberalisation. Famous writers such as Hemmingway often spoke of Spain, its beauty, its struggles and its triumphs.

Speaking of painting a picture, there are quite a lot of famous Catalan artists. Some of the more notable, being Pablo Picasso, Salvador Dalí and Antoni Gaudí; from whom the city takes the majority of its inspiration.

With motion pictures or films, a very famous Spanish director, Pedro Almodóvar, captures the reality of living as a Spaniard in some of the quirkiest and imaginative situations. If you are fine with reading subtitles, I urge you to give some of his work a view! If you want something in English which with fire up your Spanish passion, then 'Vicky, Christina, Barcelona' is a good one to get you into the swing of it.

2. MONEY, CURRENCY & ADVICE

A very important subject for any traveller: cost. Barcelona doesn't have to be an expensive city at all, as long as you aren't afraid to stray from the beaten path.

The currency is the Euro, and as much as we all want to get the best rates possible, sometimes it can be difficult to predict. Usually, changing up your money abroad gives you a better exchange, however, from my personal experience, people who have visited me with cash and changed it up have gotten worse deals than me, sometimes even losing money.

The way I manage my money is with a top up debit card that provides free withdrawals and transactions abroad. There are some that are available from places like post offices and newsagents, although these are generally single trip use. I recommend Monzo, or Revolut; both of which are free bank accounts (Revolut requires a top-up of at least 10 GBP to order a physical card), which have no fees to use abroad and generally have very reasonable rates. As they are bank accounts, you can even have wages paid to them and in case they get lost, you can freeze them instantly from your phone. This makes everything really simple for you and less stressful before departure.

3. BRING A MONEY WALLET/SMALL CONCEALABLE PURSE

This goes hand-in-hand with the last point. Barcelona, like any city (although seemingly more in recent years), has pickpockets, and if you look like a tourist; you will be a prime target.

One way to prevent this is to buy a simple money wallet which you wear under your t-shirt or under the waist of your shorts or skirt. These are comfortable, breathable in hot weather, often waterproof and very discreet. This means that you don't have to carry notes, coins or cards in your pockets or in a bulky wallet or purse. As it is well hidden and close on your person, anybody who would try to frisk any goods out of you would be sorely disappointed.

4. MAKE SURE TO BRING ENOUGH MONEY

In line with money again, it's a good idea to take more than what you would expect to spend. As I mentioned, Barcelona doesn't have to be an expensive city, but you need to take into mind the kind of trip you are wanting to take. If you want to do all the touristic activities you can, you will want enough for entry and for souvenirs; so, make sure to plan for that! But if you want a holiday of walking, wandering, exploring and adventuring; then you will only need money for food (this is assuming you have accommodation already).

The main reason you may want to bring a little extra with you is to take the train to one of the other beautiful locations in Catalonia, all within a very short distance from Barcelona. None are expensive to get to, but all will have different activities and experiences you can pay to do.

I recommend Sitges, Montserrat and Salou; of which I will discuss in more detail a little later.

5. WHEN TO VISIT

Barcelona, being in a similar latitudinal location to the UK, can make the weather a little unpredictable. It does tend to be sunny more often than not, however, the weather can change quite rapidly, and it tends to go on the more extreme scale of weather than England (i.e. Hotter in summer than the UK and colder in winter than the UK) so make sure you take a sweater just in case.

In terms of timing for tourist activity and prices, anytime from the beginning of March, all the way through to October tends to be the open tourist season, peaking in the summer holiday months of June to the end of August. Spring is a good time to go, as it starts to warm up enough that it is pleasant, but that there aren't hundreds of tourists everywhere, making queues longer and slowing up transport.

6. OUT OF SEASON TOURIST TRAVEL

Something to take note of if you do decide to go out of tourist season is that certain modes of transport only run during this time. Notably, transport to Mount Tibidabo.

This is my favourite spot in Barcelona. It is the highest point with the best views, but it doesn't give you horrible vertigo when you look down, thanks to its widespread range.

There is a very convenient uphill tram which takes you right to the top, accessible from Av. De Tibidabo (Line 7 from Catalunya, which won't make much sense now, but it will a few points from now) by bus. However, this is only convenient if you go in tourist season, otherwise, the route is a little convoluted; be sure to check online for running times beforehand.

As well as this, check any of the attractions you want to see for their opening times as well, as these may differ season-to-season.

7. BRING COMFORTABLE SHOES

Barcelona is basically situated on a slope, going from flat (at the beach) to the top of Mount Tibidabo in a slow and then rapidly escalating gradient; chances are you will walk a lot and quite often going up a very slight hill. Whether this is a shopping holiday, a sightseeing holiday or a relaxing holiday, a good, comfortable pair of shoes should definitely be included in your luggage; you can thank me later.

8. SO, WHY BARCELONA?

History aside, this city is simply breathtaking. Gaudí, an immensely talented and famous artist and architect, has inspired near enough the entire aesthetic of Barcelona. Everything is inspired by nature and the organic-ness of the Earth, but with subtle hints of decoration taken from the art deco movement. If La Sagrada Familia doesn't make your jaw drop or you gasp in wonder, then you might need to get your eyes tested!

Harrison Callaghan

It is a city of two worlds that shouldn't work, yet they run so smoothly together that it makes an incredible harmony. I am talking about the strong and rich history of the Catalonian people and the oppression they faced under the regime of Francisco Franco up until not that long ago. Considering the young age of the metropolitan wave that burst from Barcelona, the two contrasts of strong firm tradition and modern artistic vision have had to grow and develop simultaneously, making a culmination of passion, energy and emotion which I believe can be felt in every street.

The food is incredible, the people are chatty and friendly, and it is the perfect combination of being big enough to lose yourself in, but small enough to know it like the back of your hand.

So, the more important question, is why not?

9. WHERE TO STAY

So now that you have decided to visit Barcelona, it is important to know where to stay. The idea of staying in the centre (AKA Las Ramblas), may seem like an appealing concept, but it can be noisy and a little more prone to pick pockets at night. Spaniards tend to go out later than other countries, often not actually heading out until around ten in the evening. This means at one moment everything will seem calm and then it will get very busy. In my experience, practically anywhere is a safe bet in Barcelona, as in terms of size, Barcelona is a small city and you can be from one side to the other in around twenty-five minutes by metro. Catalunya is the main square and the best place to use as a bearing point to orient yourself from. My advice would be to try avoiding hotels if you want the true experience, and I will talk a little more about potential options later on.

The left side of Eixample (pronounced Ey-cham-pluh), a district just North of the centre (Catalunya), is fairly inexpensive to stay in and has some nice private hostels and shared hostels for students and backpackers. It is also the gay district of the city, so this can be a good area to stay in if you are looking to feel safer in your foreign environment.

El Raval (El Rah- bal), is the area which contains Las Ramblas and Plaça Catalunya, as well as the gothic quarter and Barceloneta (The beach). These are probably the 'down the middle' locations, fairly pricey yet on the reasonable side of it. A good hotel chain in this area is H-10.

Then there is the 'W' hotel and the 'Grand Florida'. Both are very expensive and very luxurious, so these would be best for special occasions or if you want to treat yourself to a well-deserved break.

10. STAYING SAFE

As aforementioned, pickpockets can be an issue, especially in peak times but if you have a money wallet and you take the time to perhaps study the streets near to your accommodation first on a map; you will save yourself from looking too much like a tourist and save yourself the nuisance of being targeted.

This, however, isn't the only thing to take into consideration. The road system in Barcelona is a little crazy and hard to gauge. At certain traffic lights, cars will stop completely at a red light, but quite often they will drive through them if no one is on them; this includes when the green pedestrian sign is signalling us to go. My advice, be extra caution and if in doubt, walk down the road a little further to a less busy area. With the independence of Catalonia constantly being debated, it is not unusual to see protests, and the media always seems to love to over dramatize things. In these instances, the protests are generally peaceful, and what the news calls 'riots' are just Spaniards being loud (which incidentally they are very good at.) So, don't let the talk of local protests and 'riots' put you off this amazing city; if there were real riots, they would look like real riots.

Finally, needless to say, if you go out to experience the nightlife, make sure to get certified black and yellow taxis back to your accommodation and keep an eye on your drinks. This is, of course, applicable to any city, and it is shameful to still be dealing with in 2018 but stay vigilant so as not to spoil your trip!

11. BASIC PHRASES TO LEARN: SPANISH & CATALAN

It is common courtesy to learn a few phrases and words before you go abroad; especially for English speakers. We have unfortunately earned an infamously bad reputation for being ignorant holiday goers, by expecting the world to speak English; this is not the case. A saying I have always told myself and others who ask me why I study languages is: "How can I be expected to learn about a country, without being able to speak to the people from it?"

Nearly no one can articulate themselves perfectly in more than one or two languages, there is usually one which is stronger, so grasping someone's true thoughts, feelings and meanings can be so much more meaningful when they can say it in their own tongue. Now, I'm not expecting you to get a degree in languages before you go, and having to learn how to say hello etc. can feel a little patronising to your developed and extensive adult vocabulary, but Spaniards love to see tourists try and they really appreciate it (they are also very complimentary, so it helps with the nerves).

Here are some key words and phrases in both Spanish and Catalan.

Hello: Hola (SPA/CAT)

How are you?: Cómo estás? (SPA), Com estàs? (CAT)

Fine, Thank You: Bien gracias (SPA), Molt bé, gràcies (CAT)

Good Morning: Buenos Días (SPA), Bon Dia (CAT)

Good afternoon: Buenas Tardes (SPA), Bona Tarda (CAT)

Good Evening/Night: Buenas Noches (SPA), Bona Nit (CAT)

Thank You: Gracias (SPA), Gràcies (CAT)

Yes: Sí (SPA/CAT)

Harrison Callaghan

No: No (SPA/CAT)

Do you speak English?: Hablas Inglés? (SPA), Parles Anglès? (CAT)

Help!: Ayuda (SPA), Ajuda (CAT)

See you later: Hasta Luego (SPA), Fins després (CAT)

Goodbye: Adios (SPA), Adeu (CAT)

Hopefully, you won't need to know much more than these for now, as these are only for you to throw into a conversation to be polite and to show cultural appreciation. There are plenty of videos online for pronunciation and if you are staying in the country for an extended period of time, consider taking one of the many language courses around the city in both Spanish and Catalan.

12. USEFUL APPS TO DOWNLOAD BEFORE YOU GO

Money wise, as mentioned previously, Monzo or Revolut are great account providers if you want to avoid foreign fees, so I do recommend either one of them or one similar. I would also make sure that you subscribe to your most up-to-date online banking service with your usual bank, as this can be handy in any unexpected situations.

Transport wise, Google maps works fairly well and accurately to get you where you want to go. The added benefit to this in app form is that if travelling alone and using headphones, it can direct you without having to take your phone out and make yourself more tempting to pickpockets. Apple maps are equally as efficient, so feel free to use whichever is easiest for you.

Language apps are really fun and also a great precursor to getting used to different cultures as well. The top ones used on my phone are:

- Duolingo: This is a cute little app which progresses you through words and then through phrases to help you go from beginner to intermediate. A little knowledge is useful beforehand on verb conjugations, but it's not necessary.

- Linguee: Is useful for looking up very specific things, which translation services such as Google Translate tend to get very wrong. Linguee scans the web and finds examples of that word or phrase in reports and books and then translates it to whatever language you need. The examples are used by a native in the correct context, meaning you can learn how to as well.

- Memrise: This is probably the best one, and the most engaging and challenging, however, this one does cost to have ALL of the fun features. The free version is enough for beginner levels and if you only want a few activities, but if you're like me and are language obsessed, then this is a great investment, with different packages to suit different budgets. I recommend the Japanese, it's great fun!

My final app recommendations are general ones which can be very useful. These are as follows:

Camscanner: a free app which you can use to take photos of documents and it transfers it to a scanner-like print, which is clear enough and accurate enough to be used in applications etc. This is especially handy if you need photos of visas, passports and identification cards.

Airline apps: Such as Easyjet, British Airways or any others. These can be a great way of keeping all your travel documents together and easier to keep with you.

HelloTalk: This one is more for people who are travelling alone, looking to move there or staying for an extended period of time...or if you are just very sociable! This is where you can have language exchanges with people from any country in any language and make friends before you go. It has a very effective in-app translator, so you don't have to know a word, to begin with. It also has lots of great marking features to help you and your pen-pal to learn together. I have made some great friends through this, so I do recommend it!

13. REMEMBER

This is just my little moment to give you the last-minute reminders before you set off because from this point all my tips will be for when you get there! So be sure to remember:
- Travel documents…obviously
- Appropriate clothes for the time of year
- Travel adapters for your devices
- Money wallet, Currency card and this book!

Most importantly, remember to enjoy yourself and to not be afraid to go off the beaten track every now and then

And with that, let's go!

14. ARRIVAL: AIRPORT TO CITY CENTRE

If you are coming from the UK, then you are most likely going to fly into terminal two. If you are flying with Easyjet, you will be coming from building C which means you will have to walk a little. If you are coming with any other company, then you will come out of either building A or B; directly outside A and B, there is a bus stop, where there is nearly always a light blue bus waiting; this is the Aerobus. If you come out of building C, you just walk forward across the car drop off area when you exit and follow the path going with the main road, this will bring you to buildings A and B (both within about a two-minute walk).

If you are coming from another destination, you will come out at terminal one. Don't panic, the same rules apply, but there is no A, B and C building; you just come outside and look for the Aerobus stop.

Regarding Aerobus, you can either buy your ticket at the automatic kiosk at the bus stop or from the driver. They all speak English, so don't panic if you haven't wanted to learn any Spanish before you go. (If you want to give it a go, a single is an 'ida' (ee-dah), and a return is an 'ida y vuelta'' (ee-dah-ee-vwel-ta)).

The tickets are usually around six euros for a single and eleven for a return. I highly recommend the return if you are staying for two weeks, as you have up to fifteen days to use the return. You will most likely want to go to the end of the line, to Plaça Catalunya, your new favourite starting location for anything in Barcelona, however, do check where your hotel is online before, as it may be easier for you to get off a stop earlier. Make sure you pick up a free map as well, as there are usually discount vouchers inside for tourists.

On your way back, go from Plaça Catalunya where it drops you off and simply get on the same bus back. Make sure you pick T1 or T2 for the correct terminal though!

15. THE METRO & GETTING AROUND

The Barcelona metro is thankfully very simple, and the transport payments are almost as easy. In any station, if you look for the (generally) red ticket machines and look on the screen anywhere for something called a 'T-10', you will be golden!

A T-10, generally around ten euros, counts as ten separate journeys; this includes any swaps needed and separate modes of transport within an hour. It will print your journeys on the back, so you can keep track, but if the ink is faded, it will tell you as you go through any barrier. These can also be used on buses and trams, when in doubt, just look what the locals are doing!

NB: Don't panic if there are no red ticket machines, most of them will still sell a T-10 regardless of the area, the only modes of transport that don't count with your T-10, are the cable cars, the peak-time mountain tourist tram and the Aerobus.

The Metro itself is just a number and colour system that goes back forth between two final destinations, and maps can be found anywhere, if you are truly lost, try asking, Spaniards are generally quite friendly, and most can speak at least basic English.

For attractions, I will include what line they can be found on going forward.

16. BICING

And no, that's not a spelling mistake. 'Bicing' is the name of the rent a bike service across the city which you can use as an alternative mode of travel if you are feeling adventurous! They have docking stations around the city, similar to the Santander bikes in London, so make sure to put them back to avoid extra charges.

Unfortunately, these are only for use of people with a National Identity number which you can receive if you are staying more than 3 months, however, don't despair, you can still hire bikes from around the city for reasonable prices if you are only staying for a holiday duration. They even offer Segway tours if you are feeling really adventurous.

17. TRY AND AVOID HOTELS

So, as I mentioned earlier, I would talk about why avoiding hotels can be a really great alternative for your travels. Firstly, generally, it can be cheaper to look for a private hostel, which means you can stay in nicer areas for cheaper. I have done this several times with my fiancé and they have all been very clean, helpful and in great locations, so they really aren't as scary as people think.

Obviously, if you are going for a luxury 'treat yo' self!' kind of holiday, then it is more than ok to opt for that too! I have done on special occasions and the high-end ones are seriously not to be scoffed at.

My recommendation if you feel brave enough is to try looking through (accredited) websites such as Airbnb or Couch-Hopper, to find an apartment to rent for your time abroad. If you shop around, you can find stunning flats at super reasonable prices, in ideal places; this is a great option if going with a few people. You get your own kitchen, so you can have cheaper evenings if you want to, and you don't have to share your space with anyone other than who you have chosen to go away with! To put into perspective, as a student, to stay in the student accommodation in Barcelona, it was around five hundred euros a month for a room with a shared bathroom. For the same price, I moved in with a classmate from London to a really lovely apartment in the North of Barcelona, just as the foot of the mountains, with a balcony, an exercise room and a spare bed! So, it really is worth it!

18. BOTTLED WATER

Speaking of when you get to your accommodation, wherever you pick, I would recommend stopping off at a local shop and stocking up on some bottled water. Technically, the water in Spain is treated and drinkable, but if you are used to a certain type of water, it can take you a while to adjust. If you are staying indefinitely or for an extended period, then tap water is fine, but otherwise, save yourself the stomach irritation! If you can find a supermarket near your accommodation, and you are comfortable to carry it, I would suggest going for the five litre bottles, as you can pick one up for usually under a euro and it will most likely last you a week, unless you drink like me and need a five litre bottle every other day!

19. GROCERIES

If renting an apartment or even if you just want some snacks for the evenings when you get back from exploring (or if you haven't bought water yet), I recommend familiarising yourself with any local supermarkets and stock up! Minibars can be great for convenience, but they can cost extortionate amounts, so if you can prepare in advance, you may save your wallet in the long run.

Barcelona also has some amazing markets (which I will mention later), so even just going for their incredible fresh produce can be a really special treat.

20. COME WITH AN EMPTY STOMACH

Barcelona has some incredible food! Spanish food is very underrated in my opinion and has one of the nicest pallets of flavours that the Mediterranean has to offer. Spain is very big on flavour and very big on fresh. If you go anywhere, you can guarantee that the produce will likely come from one of the famous city markets, or if it's seafood, probably from their own bays and harbours.

Really embody the Spanish and Catalan lifestyle, by taking tapas (or pinxos 'pinchos' in the North) with drinks. Firstly, this stops you getting too intoxicated too quickly and allows you to enjoy yourself for longer, and secondly, they make for a delightful little taster of Spanish and Catalan culture with each drink.

It is quite a 'young vibe' sort of place, but it is really tasty and quite a fun and crazy experience, but if you get the chance, go and try '100 montaditos'. A 'montadito' is basically just a small sandwich, and this place has one hundred different fillings. There are vegetarian, options, but unfortunately, they don't have vegan sandwiches, but they have some great sides as well!

The prices are ridiculously cheap, and they are tasty and filling. I would say 4-5 is more than enough per person. Don't make the mistake that my flatmate, her sister and I did, by ordering 40 euros worth between the three of us; to put into perspective, most of them are one euro each (Wednesdays and Sundays, everything actually is a euro).

21. FISH-LOVER'S HEAVEN

One thing is certainly undeniable, if you love seafood, you will adore the food in Barcelona. Everything is so fresh and delicious, to the point that most of the things are still alive on the iced displays. Most of the fish in the city is brought in from just out to sea and brought back into Barcelona bay that morning. Having had this availability to such great fish for such a long time, there are many seasoned chefs who have perfected cooking stunning fish dishes.

For the best authentic and fusion paella that I have tasted, be sure to visit Arròs i Peix, a swanky looking, yet surprisingly cheap restaurant about two minutes from Jaume I station (Line 4, The Yellow Line). They have a little fish stall just as you go in, where you pick the fish you want, fresh from the ice, most still moving! All the staff speak English, Spanish and Catalan, so they can explain everything to you; and don't panic if you don't like fish, my friend had one with chicken and they said it was delicious.

For its swanky interior, we paid around 100 Euros between eight of us, and that included a large shared started of calamari and a bottle of wine!

22. STREET FOOD

Street food isn't really a thing per se, but they do offer a lot of markets with incredible hand food which can be taken on-the-go or eaten at the counter with other patrons. Probably the best example of this is La Boqueria on La Rambla.

It is about half way down on the right-hand side and has big black gates with a cross above it. Delve straight in and wonder through all the stalls. It starts with sweets, and then onto meats and cheeses and then on to eggs, fish and then all the snack foods and fresh juices you can imagine. One thing I definitely recommend is a Spanish empanada, which I incidentally learned is very different to Latin American empanadas. Spanish ones are more like puff pastry, filled with chunky Mediterranean vegetables and often either chicken or tuna, are delicious and surprisingly filling. Latin American ones, as cooked for me by my Colombian flatmate, as more like Jamaican style patties you find in West-

Indian supermarkets, and are usually filled with potato, minced beef, onion and a little chilli; equally delicious, yet completely different flavours.

If that is something you want to try, it isn't street food as such (as it is a sit-in restaurant), but there is a great mini chain of Colombian restaurants in Barcelona, where you can have some delicious traditional Colombian meals. Caution, come with an empty stomach and a hearty appetite, as the food portions are large, and their staple ingredients are very filling! The chain is called Tropicalissima, which is nice and cost effective, but it is clear that everyone who goes there is Latin American and can generally only speak Spanish, so this may only be an option for the brave and more experienced Spanish traveller.

23. SWEET CRAVINGS

Valor… it is a must! Valor is a brand of Spanish chocolate, which is deep and rich and delicious; and I am honestly not a chocolate fan! The one I know of is just behind the official Cathedral of Barcelona, in the Gothic Quarter. It is a small café sized shop, and it can have a tendency to get very busy, very quickly. They have a menu inspired by chocolate in everything, so there is something bound to take your fancy. If like me, you aren't so much about the sweet, they offer a range of sandwiches (without chocolate) and you can always indulge in a chocolate milkshake or latté.

If chocolate isn't your thing, there is a delicious ice cream parlour near Jaume I station (Line 4) called Chocolat-Box, which is open until late and sells an amazing selection of very creamy and luxurious ice creams at a lower price tag.

24. DRINKS, DRINKS, DRINKS

Spain (and generally most of Europe) is well known for its cheap alcohol, particularly wine, as a great deal of it is grown there. If you like red wine, you pretty much can't go wrong with even their cheapest rioja, as the region is about an hour's drive away! I have walked through La Rioja region on the way of Saint James, and it is beautiful, but more importantly, when you were walking all day and living on a budget of around eight euros a day, it was a delight to know that I could buy a whole bottle of rioja for around 1 Euro, and incidentally, it was rather delicious.

If you want to go big and do the tourist thing on your first night, then take a stroll down la rambla and maybe stop off in a few bars, it's a great atmosphere in the evening when all the Spaniards come out. There is a great bar with an outdoor seating area about half-way down with giant mojitos. Unfortunately, I had already had a couple of drinks when I first went there on New Year's Eve, so I don't remember the name of it, however, you won't miss it; the mojito jugs are twice the size of your head, and generally, everyone is having one! They are a bit pricey, mine was 20 Euros, but this may be a seasonal price, but to make you feel a bit better about the price...Spaniards definitely aren't stingy with the booze!

Just drink responsibly...

25. FUN BAR AND NIGHT OUT EXPERIENCES

Two of the most fun and quirky experiences I have had in Barcelona have come to me from stumbling upon them by accident. The first one 'El Bosc de las fades' or 'The Fairy Forest' is a well-hidden bar at the end of La Rambla, and it is other worldly… There is an actual forest inside of it for starters, as well as statues of fairies, caves, water features, a bizarre room of circus and folklore style paintings and wax figures, and even thunder and lightning! It is quite dark inside for dramatic effect, but if you want light, you can sit in the circus room. Besides the novelty of all of this, they also make some mean cocktails which are absolutely delicious, and deadly; all at very reasonable prices.

The second is a little less (or more) tame than 'El Bosc' (depending on how you want to look at it); this is called 'Chupitos' or quite literally 'Shots'. Don't get discouraged straight away, they sell normal drinks too, but, as you probably guessed, they specialise in the little glasses, of which I believe they have more than 600 different ones! There are a few of them around Barcelona, one of the ones I went in had all the names written on the walls and you could be brave and simply point at one. If you are a little cowardly (like me) you can ask the friendly bar staff for a couple and ask them to start off gentle with you!

For some extra hilarity, if you want to embarrass a friend or relative, ask them to prepare a 'Monica Lewinsky', a little more expensive, but a lot of fun! I won't say any more than that but have a video camera ready!

26. HOW TO TACKLE LA RAMBLA

Now I have mentioned this thing a few times, and I assume you have heard of Las Ramblas; the most famous street in all of Barcelona, however, if you don't, it is a very long road filled with little stalls and boutiques, restaurants and cafés which all lead down to the harbour. It is a pleasant walk to do and there are some not-to-miss things to do down here, such as 'La Boqueria' one of Barcelona's oldest and most famous markets, and the erotic museum just opposite, often with a live actress of Marilyn Monroe waving from the window above.

Now, I mentioned that I assumed you knew of Las Ramblas, and you have probably been thinking, 'well why has this author been writing La Rambla consciously all this time?'; well simply, because there is only one! Adding 's' at the end of things in Spanish pluralises things like in English. As there is only one, the Catalan and Spanish natives from the city refer to it as the singular; why they have never just changed the name is a mystery to me.

Tackling it is fairly simple, just stroll at your own pace, take in the stalls that interest you and politely decline the campaigners offering to give you discount at bars or 'Dutch cafés', unless that is what you have come for. Other than that, it is just a very long boulevard with some interesting sites to see. Definitely have a look at La Boqueria and other markets nearby as mentioned before, as these are really fascinating.

27. MINI CAMDEN

This isn't a technical name for this area, rather a self-named area I like to visit with my fiancé. If you come out the metro station at Plaça Catalunya (Lines 1 and 3) at the 'Las Ramblas' exit, then you will be facing straight down the iconic Las Ramblas. As you start to walk down it, on your right you will see a fast food place called 'Pans & Company', with a road leading to the right just before it; this is the beginning of what I like to call Mini Camden.

If you have never been to Camden in London, it is an amalgamation of punk and rock shops, tattoo shops, weird and wonderful clothing shops, vinyl record stores (where my fiancé likes to drag me) and some unique restaurants. It doesn't just go down this road, you reach a little junction at one point, and you can take any of the directions and be certain to find something fun and punk-esque.

28. GOTHIC QUARTER

I mentioned the Gothic Quarter very briefly before when talking about the Cathedral of Barcelona and Valor chocolate café, but this is effectively the stunning area between La Rambla (Metro station Liceu Line 3) and Jaume I (line 4), the two areas I have spoken about already. These small winding streets decorated with spires of gothic inspiration, arches and pillars with intricate designs etched into them, this is easily one of the more architecturally beautiful areas of Barcelona.

If you get the opportunity, then I would take the tour of the Cathedral, as it is very beautiful inside; the gothic touches adding a melancholy and grandiose feel to the interior.

29. ESCAPE ROOMS

This is an awesome experience and Barcelona is really famous for them! These are activities you do with a group of friends or family where you get locked in a big room and have to solve a mystery in a certain time to get let out (don't worry, they aren't going to keep you in there if you don't complete it!). I did one with 7 other friends and we had a blast, it is full of riddles, physical activities and puzzles, so there is stuff there for everyone! It is an absolute must for a good laugh, and I would advise booking in advance.

30. FLAMENCO? IN BARCELONA?

For people who travel to Spain often, this one may make you scratch your heads, as Flamenco comes from the South of Spain; so, what is it doing in a Northern city which doesn't even like to fully call itself Spanish? Simple, Flamenco is amazing and powerful to watch and is generally loved by everyone. Granted, you won't just see Flamenco singers, dancers and musicians everywhere in Barcelona like you may a bit more frequently in the South, but there are many shows on in the evenings with some great acts. Flamenco music is also on the rise again in popularity within popular music. If it is something that interests you, look up these favourite Flamenco inspired singers and musicians of mine:

- Rosalía
- Pablo Alborán
- Estrella Morente

Harrison Callaghan

- El Niño de Elche

Enjoy!

31. ARTISTS OF BARCELONA

It's hard to come to Barcelona and not experience the art, whether that was your intention of the trip or not; it's everywhere! And even if you don't think that you like art, or know any artists, it's important to know the scope of the artists that Spain has produced.

Pablo Picasso for one was born in the South of Spain in Málaga, however, one of his museums is situated in Barcelona, in the El Born area, fairly near to Jaume I (Line 4).

Salvador Dalí, the godfather of surrealism and famous for his quirkiness in general. You can see much of his influence in the sculptures around the city made by modern artists in homage to the art movement. If you want to explore his world, you can travel by train (RENFE: an over ground service out of the city from Plaça Catalunya) to Figueres and visit the Dalí Museum Theatre, which showcases films and pieces of his work throughout. Dalí himself is even buried in the crypt under the stage!

Antoní Gaudí, I can't even begin to summarise his influence in one paragraph, so I shall save it for the next tip.

Paco Rabanne is a fashion designer of Basque origin (which is fairly close to Catalunya and shares the border with France across the Pyrenees) and is most famous across the world for his fragrances for men and women, including One Million, Invictus, Lady Million and Olympéa.

Some famous actors and actresses have come out of Spain as well and can often be celebrated in Barcelona at film festivals and are used in many famous Spanish films. Penelope Cruz, Javier Bardem and Antonio Banderas being particularly notable as actors who have crossed the borders of American films and British films alike. Even Millie Bobby Brown of Stranger Things was born in Málaga Spain!

So, if you thought you knew no artists from Spain, now you do.

32. GAUDI, GAUDI, GAUDI

"If you could bring back any famous person from history to have a conversation with, who would you choose?"

This is a hard question for anyone, including me, but I have to say that one of my top competitors for that spot would be the man who dreamed up the streets of my favourite city and effectively captured my heart; Antoní Gaudí. You won't be able to go anywhere in the city without finding something inspired by, or directly designed by him.

He started off fairly traditionally, however, as his influence grew and his playful introduction to the Art Nouveau movement started gaining notoriety, his designs became ever lavish and ever astounding. In order of tameness, here are some of his buildings and works you have to see.

Casa Calvet
Even though this was a later piece, it was commissioned to be in a Baroque style, with very classic French style balconies and façades. The

balcony shape, however, did act as a precedent for the balcony shape in his later work Casa Batlló.

Palau Güell

This was the residential home of his family, and although it doesn't look very much like any other Gaudí pieces from outside, it makes up for it inside with large glass domes built into the ceiling.

Casa Vicens

This was another commissioned work, but this time for a ceramics company. This was Gaudí's first big commissioned piece, yet it ended up being more of a foreshadowing of his growing style than some of his later projects. The use of ceramic in particular ways amongst the façades perhaps being a direct inspiration to the 'trencadis' or mosaic style design that Gaudí favoured.

Casa Batlló

This was a building which was up for a renovation that he ended up taking over and designing. Originally it was not liked by the city as it violated many of the guidelines which described how buildings must be, but nowadays it is celebrated as a piece which in essence became the first in a long line of Gaudiesque architecture.

Casa Milà or La Pedrera

Harrison Callaghan

This was the last private residential housing that Gaudí designed. Here it is clear to see the coming together of all the ideas previous to this, which include La Sagrada Familia and Parc Güell, however, these are immeasurably grander.

Parc Güell

Located on top of a steep hill, Parc Güell looks out across Barcelona, but hidden amongst the trees are gorgeous stone pillars, encrusted with stones, and the famous 'trencadis' design absolutely everywhere. In the main area, you can see two more of the houses he designed, which are somewhat comparable to St Basil's Cathedral in Moscow in shape and design.

La Sagrada Familia

This is the pièce de résistance of all of his work. I know that I have been transfixed with this building since I was about six, and even have a tattoo of it on my arm, but this building makes even the most unreactive of people tend to gasp. Coming out of the station and seeing it is indescribable but going inside is otherworldly. I cannot begin to explain it all to you here, so it will be the penultimate tip to offer you.

33. EXPLORE MORE THAN JUST THE CENTRE

This is a fairly vague concept, as there isn't really much of a centre to Barcelona, it is more a case of lots of big tourist attractions and main shopping districts and streets, dotted around the city sporadically, so you are never truly far from something of interest.

In Eixample, you have probably the most in terms of tourist attractions, as well as El Raval and Plaça Espanya/ Montjuïc; so, if you want to go off the beaten track a little, I would say save these areas for another day.

I recommend Barceloneta, which is the lazy paced, pretty district leading down to the beach. There are plenty of street vendors selling ice cream and cooled and refreshing beers and soft drinks for you to relax with.

El Born and La Ribera are probably about as touristy, yet out of the centre as you can get without having to travel too far. Here you have Barcelona's version of Paris' Arc de Triomphe, called…unsurprisingly, Arc de Triomf in Catalan. You also have the gorgeous park of La Ciutadella, which is a big park with sculptures, family areas, jogging areas, dog-friendly zones, Barcelona Zoo and the most important feature, Cascada, no not the electronic singer of the 2000s, but a grand and magnificent fountain of Romanesque grandeur. It is a peaceful park, so why not try taking a casual lunch down that way one day?

The Gracía district used to be a town in its own right, but now it is a fairly modern and swanky shopping district with some amazing restaurants and unique boutiques. As it is an old neighbourhood, quite a lot of the population are still elderly, which is quite an unusual contrast to the modern setting.

34. PARKS AND GARDENS

Following on from the beautiful Parc de la Ciutadella, there are absolutely loads of places to relax and unwind with a stroll or sitting under a tree with a book in Barcelona's many parks and public gardens.

Avoiding the main tourist one of Parc Güell (to be mentioned briefly later), one of my favourites is Parc Laberint d'Horta (Mundet Line 3), as it is a hidden gem that not many tourists actually know about, meaning that generally, it is quiet and only occupied by Spanish natives. As the name suggests, there is a labyrinth, or maze, in the middle of it, which is great fun for kids and adults. There are cute hidden away alcoves and seating areas if you want some down time, or just a peaceful moment with your significant other (a fun fact about this expression later in tip 48).

In Montjuïc, an area fairly near to the centre (Plaça Espanya Line 1 & 3) you have the Magic Fountain and Olympic park, which I will mention more in tip 43, but you also have the Botanic gardens, which is like walking through a huge nature reserve with its multitude of exotic plants and wild animals. This is fun for kids, but also an educational and quieter day you can schedule around your busier ones.

35. MOUNT TIBIDABO

This is probably my favourite part of the city, for many different reasons. Firstly, because it's the highest point of Barcelona and you can see the whole city (and other neighbouring cities) from the peak. Secondly, because it is lush and green and makes for a lovely hike. If you have the time to spare and want to get some clean mountain air into your lungs, then taking a walk up mount Tibidabo is one of the best walks I know. If you take the metro to Vall d'Hebron (Line 3) and open google maps, setting a location to Amusement Park Tibidabo, then it will show you the way. You can take this route, which follows the main road, but I will explain a more adventurous route later on.

Another reason I love mount Tibidabo, which I have already kind of spoilt for you, is the fact that there is an amusement park at the top. It's not a full-scale amusement park, but there is a rollercoaster, Ferris wheel, a moving look-out deck, and plenty of food, drink and indoor entertainment as well. This amusement park is only open during peak tourist times, so from around the beginning of March to the end of August.

The final, and main, reason I love this place, is the view in the evening; this is truly one of the most beautiful sights that Barcelona can offer you. The crisp cool air, carrying the scent of the Mediterranean Sea, the setting sun and the twinkling lights of the city below; it is (for me) a paradise. It is truly romantic, but it can also be awe inspiring on a personal level as well, so those travelling alone, should definitely designate time to take this trip. At the top, there is a cathedral, and you can take a lift up to the very top (the true highest point, which astoundingly, makes a massive difference to the view from at the bottom of the cathedral), and look out across the whole mountain range from any direction.

This is also where I proposed to my now fiancé, at sunset.

This may not be a deciding factor for you to go, I don't expect that it would be, but it shows that the view is so spectacular, so special, that I would choose to ask one of the biggest questions of my life in that very spot. I really hope you enjoy it as much as I do.

(Fun interesting fact: All 'Friends' fans may be scratching their heads, asking themselves why Mount Tibidabo sounds so familiar, allow me to answer this burning question. Joey uses Mount Tibidabo as his chat-up line to women, describing how he was trekking in the foothills of it. You may also remember the iconic scene where he taught Ross this story to help him on his date; feel free to have a laugh to yourself when you remember this on your trip!)

36. BARE-ALL ON THE BEACH

If you are a fan of getting an all-over summer tan, then look no further than Barcelona's main beach. It isn't specifically designated as a nudist or semi-nude beach; however, it is the general consensus in Spain and most of Western Europe that baring all on the beach isn't something to be ashamed of. If you are ever in doubt, you can always check on a local government website, which will certainly have a page available in English. Any search on beach etiquette in Europe should provide you with all the surety you will need, to release your inner free spirit and furthermore, to take advice from the popular feminist movement, free the nipple.

37. SITGES

This is probably my favourite town in Catalonia. Aside from being the gay capital of Spain and hosting some amazing festivals such as the horror film festival; it is one of the most picturesque and clean little towns you can imagine. This is a train ride from Barcelona. You take the R2S train to Sant Vincenç de Calders, which takes about forty minutes and costs somewhere around eight euros for a return (be sure to take more with you in case of price changes). The train ride becomes increasingly pretty as you leave the city until eventually, you are on tracks running practically next to the sea and cliffs. Once in Sitges, it's not difficult to find your way to the beach, as the whole town in on a hill; the station at the top and the beach at the bottom, so, just follow any road you like heading downhill and you can't go wrong. Once on the beach, you will see a gorgeous boulevard of palm trees and a long stretch of soft white sand. In summer they have deck chairs you can hire, and men will wander between selling cocktails which come delivered to your chair, just look for the men shouting mojito!

Speaking of mojito, one fun activity you can do is go and take the Barcardi museum tour. It is a surprisingly small museum, but it is more to do with the history of the brand, as the creator of the famous rum came from Sitges. You get to finish this tour off by learning how to make one of two cocktails, which you then get to go and enjoy out on the veranda.

If the party life is for you, then Sitges is definitely the place to go, as the parties in the evening are quite legendary, especially during pride week; heterosexual, homosexual or anything else, you will have a good time. What is the nicest thing, is that the general pace of the town is older and slower and more laid-back, meaning when you are likely nursing a hangover the following day, you can lead a European lifestyle and slow down, taking time to recover and appreciate the day.

38. MONSERRAT

Quite literally the opposite of Sitges in many ways, but equally charming. Instead of a beach, you are up against the side of a mountain, which you can either go up by cable car or by tram, as a man who is afraid of heights, I can assure you, the cable car is actually very pleasant. To get there, you go in the opposite way to Sitges and head inland and slightly North-West, you can go from Plaça Catalunya to Martorell Central on the R4 (powered by Renfe) and then take the R5 from there to Monistrol de Monserrat (the cable car or tram stop). This is quite a long trip to take at around an hour and a half each way, but if you are willing to take the trip, you won't be disappointed.

Montserrat itself is a monastery, which is beautifully built into the side of the mountain. There is a gorgeous cathedral, which even the non-religious can appreciate its beauty. As this is a practising cathedral, please be respectful and dress modestly and remain silent when inside the actual cathedral walls; the architecture is enough to stun you into silence anyway.

They have a nice museum with some lovely pieces of art, famous to Montserrat, as well as a few lovely restaurants. If you are feeling particularly brave, you can take a further tram to the very top and take one of the many hiking routes through the mountains to explore the ruins of the older parts of the monastery (some of which you will briefly see as you go up the cable car.

Again, this is a beautiful viewing spot, so bring a camera or plenty of charge on your phone to take photos. If you look carefully into the distance, you can even see Mount Tibidabo!

39. SALOU

Further down from Sitges, but in the same direction is Salou. This area of Tarragona is more like your classic holiday resort city, with a strip, plenty of bars, plenty of hotels and plenty of luscious beaches; that all added with a slightly milder climate, it can all seem very tempting. However, as this guide is how not to live like a tourist, maybe the only thing that would bring you here, is if you are an adrenaline junkie, or if you have children; as its main attraction is PortAventura World.

This may seem like a bit of a trek to just go to a theme park, which you could do in your own country, however here you get the sun and the beach, which when you have had a crazy morning on the rollercoasters, can be very welcoming to relax on. The city itself is clean and friendly and most people can speak at least basic English, although don't go as far as to expect it. It is an hour and a half by train from Sants over-ground station, which you can get to by metro from Plaça Catalunya, as it is on line 3 (and 5). As it is a tourist city, if worse comes to the worse a hotel or hostel for the night won't be too much, and you will have plenty of selection if it gets too late into the evening and you don't want to travel back.

40. THE CITY OF MUSIC

In Barcelona, it feels like you can always hear music. You have street performers down La Rambla, guitarists playing in secluded squares and parks and even performers on the metro (sometimes more frequently than you'd like), but their biggest area of music, is live music; regardless, it's hard to say that Barcelona hasn't got 'soul'.

Harrison Callaghan

There are a plethora of different concert halls dotted around the city, most of which tend to cater for a specific type (or types) of music. Saying this, Barcelona is a very passionate city, so they like expressive music, meaning they have a big fondness for jazz and blues music, which, as you will see is available in practically all of them!

Here are a few of the big ones:

Bikini
• Funk, Hip Hop, Contemporary Rock Concerts)

Harlem Jazz Club
• Jazz, Rock, Latin, Blues Concerts)

Jamboree
• Jazz & Blues Concerts

La Boîte
• Jazz, Blues, Funk/Soul, Salsa Concerts

La Cova del Drac, "Jazzroom"
• Jazz Concerts

London Bar
• Eclectic: rock, jazz... Concerts)

Luz de Gas
• Eclectic: Soul, Country, Salsa, Rock, Jazz, Pop Concerts

That should be more than enough to get your musical taste buds tingling! The last one in particular I recommend. Luz de Gas is a beautifully charming renovated old theatre, that has been taken care of with a lot of love. The music played in there sounds fantastic, and I had the best experience watching one of my favourite artists, Susanne Sundfør, perform as an extra surprise for my fiancé, the day after I proposed; it truly is really beautiful.

41. FESTIVALS

With Barcelona being so big on live music, it is unsurprising that there are absolutely loads of festivals that are held around the city throughout the year. One of the biggest and most notable of which is the Primavera festival, held at the end of Spring. This festival showcases new and rising talent from around the world, paired on the same stages as bigger acts, to provide the chance for up-and-coming artists to get themselves known. I got to see a mini stage set up for this down at Barceloneta, and it was really very good, I am definitely making plans to go and see it fully myself as soon as I can! The fun thing about Primavera is you can basically start buying tickets for the next one, as soon as one is done. They do this to promote you to come for the overall music experience and not just the big artists, even including a massive reduction in ticket prices before the set-list is put up. If you are an audiophile and absolutely love music, then what are you still doing sat there reading this? Go and have a look!

What I love about Barcelona as well, is that they always try to support and promote local talent, rising talent and to reinforce traditional practice. This means there are also festivals just dedicated to guitar in all of its forms, as well as a Flamenco festival, to help strengthen the roots of Spanish and Catalonian tradition.

Being the best place in Spain to go for a music festival, there is bound to be one to suit your music tastes, you have even already heard of some.

42. NIGHT LIFE

This is one area, which as a British student, I should be more familiar with; however, I am considered an old man in a young man's body, so it only happens on rare occasion, however, I will say that the nights I have had out in Barcelona have been some of the most fun I have had when going out.

Although mentioned above as a concert venue, Razzmatazz is a very well-known club with five massive rooms, catering to all different music tastes, and if you are a student on exchange, they sometimes offer student nights at cheaper rates. Razzmatazz is more of an all-rounder if you are looking for a myriad of different styles and flavours of music.

If the reason you avoid clubs like me is that it gets too hot inside, then Barcelona has you covered. Probably the nicest experience is La Terrrazza (yes there are three "R's"), which is an open-air night club in Poble Espanyol, or the Older Spanish Village. This is a somewhat classier experience (I use the term lightly), as entry fees do include a drink and you can book to be on the guest list in advance to make your fees cheaper on the day. It mainly specialises in

Techno, Electronic and Trance music, but it has been known to have some more chilled one-off events.

43. PLACES TO SEE

I have mentioned a lot of these already, but here is a short but comprehensive list of some of the places you absolutely have to see; if I haven't mentioned them already, or they will be mentioned soon, I will point that out.

-    La Sagrada Familia:

My absolute favourite place in the universe; it has its own chapter coming up.

-    Fira Montjuïc:

The 'magical' fountain of Montjuïc, which dances and lights up to famous tracks such as Queen's 'Barcelona', do be sure to check their times and days online, as these change throughout the year.

-    Recinte Modernista de Sant Pau:

This is the former grand hospital of Barcelona, designed by none other than the wonderful Antoní Gaudí. Nowadays, much like Gaudí's other houses, it is used as an architectural display of his immense vision of art and nature- a well-worth visit.

-    Gaudí's houses:

Speaking of Gaudí's houses, these shouldn't be missed off of your list, as each one has its own unique style and vision, and each is as visually titillating as the last.

- Mount Tibidabo:

As mentioned before, an absolute must.

- El Bosc de las fades:

The quirky indoor forest bar I mentioned before is definitely worth the visit, just to say you have sipped cocktails in a bar within a hidden cave or forest with waterfalls.

- Parc Güell:

I skipped this earlier as it is a 'main' tourist attraction, however, it is still absolutely gorgeous and is worth the visit. You book tickets for the main area in time slots, which you can do either online or at the Parc itself, whichever suits you. You can appreciate the park for free, however, if you have fallen in love with the work of Gaudí (which by now I hope you have), you will want to see the beautiful structures he has created. To get to Parc Güell, take line 3 to Lesseps and then follow the signs for Parc Güell, this will take to the bottom of a very steep hill leading up to it, but worry not, as Barcelona city council has installed escalators in the streets to take you up. If you do have trouble walking or have any disabilities, there is an easier access route from Vallcarca (same line).

(fun fact for all those die-hard America's Next Top Model fans, the final for the very first cycle had its fashion show performed down the curved stone corridor, see if you can find it!)

44. PICTURES YOU WILL WANT TO TAKE

Similar to places to see, however, these are photos that I think are worth the effort of either taking a professional camera if you own one or at the very least, giving yourself extra time in, to make the most of it.

Firstly, La Sagrada Familia, again I will talk about this more in a few tips from now, but you will want to take a camera.

Montserrat is extremely beautiful and is situated right next to a massive glacial valley, which makes the views, with its sweeping horizon, permeated with the remaining jagged peaks; truly breath-taking.

Recinte Modernista de Sant Pau, the old city hospital, is now brimming with gardens and courtyards of a true European feel and make for some gorgeous photos in the afternoon sun.

Mount Tibidabo is a place where I feel it impossible to get a bad picture, as every angle of it reveals something else in this city. Whether it is the large gold statue of Jesus above the cathedral, reminiscent of Cristo Redentor in Rio de Janeiro, or the padlocks of all the lovers who have looked out at the city from the little look out deck (yes that includes me), there are photo opportunities everywhere.

Sitges has the kind of white stone houses and small winding streets which make you think of beach towns and sunsets in Greece. With the stunning mixture of old world buildings with their rustic feel, paired with a vibrant night life and population of all backgrounds; it paints a picture of true integration, making it very beautiful in its own right.

45. PLACES TO WALK AND STROLL

I love to walk, I mean I'd have to if I was crazy enough to walk the entirety of the country, but Barcelona has some really nice trails that you alone or you and your party can blaze, as well as quieter and lazier avenues where you can meander at a leisurely pace; here, however, are my two favourites.

As promised earlier, I will tell you about a route up to the peak of Tibidabo which is for the inner adventurer in you. It is hard work and quite steep, but it is fairly well laid out, so it isn't dangerous; caution should of course always be taken with any mountain, and if taking children or dogs, it would be wise to keep them close or on a leash (even the kids if need be!). As you come up the main road, following google maps along the side of a highway, you will eventually reach a corner turning sharply to the right. By this, there is a bench and a small post-box sized stone tower of sorts, but also, a trail about ten metres to the left of the bench; this is your trail. Over all, it cuts out about an hour of your journey taking this route, and it's a great way to get the heart pumping. Crossing the highway can be challenging and at times dangerous, be sure to walk all the way around the corner to get a clear vantage point of traffic both ways if planning to do this trail. The way is fairly self-explanatory, and when in doubt, just head upwards.

Barceloneta is a long promenade along the beach of Barcelona. If you have come from the centre and walked your way down, you will most likely come onto it from the bottom side of it. If you were to take this leisurely stroll in the late afternoon, or early evening, all the way down to the other end, there are plenty of very nice restaurants where you could stop for dinner, giving you a nice walk back afterwards to help let your food go down.

46. SHOPPING STREETS, CENTRES AND DISTRICTS

Although it's generally avoided on holiday, it is inevitably going to happen, so you might as well just go with it and enjoy yourself. Luckily, Barcelona makes this job quite easy, as whether it's sunny or cloudy (it does happen), you can be sure there is always an amazing shopping centre with plenty of your favourites and some Spanish brands and boutiques which may surprise you. As previously mentioned, they have a large 'El Corte Inglés' in Plaça Catalunya, which has tonnes to see and do inside, even if it's just a break from a spell of bad weather.

If your goal is actually shopping, then Gloriés (line 1) is a really nice area. It has a sort of Canary Warf vibe to it, but the shopping centre itself is young and vibrant, with lots of amazingly diverse restaurants and shops. One restaurant, which is a chain, but is still delicious is called Udon; if you love Wagamama or YoSushi, this will be a welcome treat. I, above everything on the menu, recommend the Ika tempura, which is effectively calamari. What makes it special is the combination of Japanese with Spanish, but having light tempura batter and Japanese mayonnaise, paired with Spanish brava sauce (think slightly spicy smoky flavour).

Diagonal is also a trendy place to go shopping, this whole massive road leads to Passeig de Gracía and eventually back to Plaça Catalunya, so you can make a whole route of it. This area specialises in more of the designer brands and the bespoke boutiques for if you are looking for something truly special.

47. SOUVENIRS TO BRING HOME

Souvenirs are a hard one to pick, as you want something unique and you want something special unless you have something you collect (fridge magnets, postcards, coaster etc.). Here are a few suggestions of what you can bring back instead which will either wow the people you are buying for, or be wonderful memories for you in years to come.

On La Rambla, you have a lot of private artists stationed, selling their artwork. These pieces are very good and often depict gorgeous scenes of Barcelona that you (and I) don't even know about. Firstly, this can be a great way to learn some new areas, but secondly, by buying these, you get something truly unique and you support local artists. If landscapes and cityscapes aren't your thing, a lot of them also do real life portraits or caricatures of you, with or without your party.

Ceramic bulls. A strange notion, but there are these small ceramic bulls which are somewhat a collector's item showcasing many artist's unique styles. We have three of them in our household, and each of them is decorated in a different way; the ones we have are a Picasso, a Kandinsky and a Joan Miró. They also have some novelty ones with Elvis and the like, so they are quite fun too. The bigger ones aren't so cheap, but they are genuine collector's items and are rather quirky and fun.

Normally you have to pick up little gifts for the family or your co-workers back in the office. Provided that neither your work colleagues nor your family back home have any nut allergies, you can't go home without trying chocolate almonds and turrón; and maybe if you are feeling generous, sharing some with them.

Turrón is Spain's answer to the Americanised French sweet, Nougat. It comes in a vast amount of flavours and textures, from crispy and hard like peanut brittle, to soft, melt-in-your-mouth gooiness. The most well-known brand is Turrons Vicens, and I highly recommend them. You can find one on the basement floor of the gargantuan 'El Corte Inglés' in Plaça Catalunya. Chocolate almonds are what they say on the tin, but they have a special recipe and are dusted with fine cocoa, making them extra indulgent. You can pick these up at La Boqueria market on La

Rambla, or even at the airport on the way home if you are desperate for a last-minute fix.

48. FUNNY LITTLE SPANISH CULTURAL QUIRKS TO LOOK OUT FOR

I thought it would be fun to share a little light on some of the really fun and cute things that Spaniards and Catalonians do habitually, which I find incredibly endearing and I hope you will too; feel free to integrate any of these into your lives or your travels to show you know the culture, or to confuse your family back home.

Now I mentioned that I would tell you a fun fact about the term 'significant other' or 'other half' in Spain. In Spain, your partner is referred to colloquially as 'My Half-Orange'. I assume you are the other half of that orange, giving it the same meaning as in English, but I am still clueless as to why it's an orange.

Probably my favourite quirk is elevator talk. Now don't freak out, it won't be a full-blown conversation in Spanish with a stranger (unless you want it to be), Spaniards and Catalonians like to greet everyone in the lift when they get in and say goodbye to everyone as they leave. This is true whether they have lived next door to you for twenty years or if they are likely never going to see you again; if you make eye contact upon entry, you say 'hola' and 'adios' accordingly. The funny thing that I find is that even if you are in that lift a long time with them; unless they think you are Spanish, they generally won't utter another word, but they still feel the need to say goodbye.

Two other quick quirks which you can use to sound like a native, are the real way to greet someone from Spain, and the common way they say goodbye. In Spanish class, or Spanish lessons (even in my little guide, sorry), they will teach you that you can say 'buenos días', 'buenas tardes' or 'buenas noches' depending on the time of day. This is true, and it is correct, however, it's a little too formal for what they are used to, saying 'buenas' alone is more than enough. Next time you enter somewhere, try saying 'hola buenas' at the checkout and watch them think you can speak Spanish. The one to say goodbye isn't so much a change of the word, or slang, but just the rushed nature in which they say it. You have probably heard of 'hasta luego' (mentioned in my mini section too), to mean 'see you later'. This is pronounced correctly as:

-ASTA-LOO-EY-GO

However, in reality, it is generally pronounced more like:

-ALOOWOGO

Which severely confused my natively Colombian flatmate, who thought everyone just had some weird trendy way of saying goodbye, of which she had been trying to copy.

One last note about cultural quirks. Don't get offended by Spanish people. When you are taught Spanish, you are taught how to speak like an English person in Spain; very polite, and well-mannered. Whereas the reality can seem a little harsh and unfriendly (sometimes even rude), but this is the true Spanish nature. Even my Colombian flatmate was horrified at first, so don't be shocked if instead of greeting you at a bar with "Hola Señora, ¿que le gustaría beber?" (Hello Madam, what would you like to drink?), they will most likely just say… "Dime" (Tell me).

49. LA SAGRADA FAMILIA

Here it is, finally enough space that I can dedicate fully to this masterpiece of a building. If you haven't gone to visit La Sagrada Familia yet whilst reading this book, then I must not have been dropping enough hints at it. This building is barely describable without tarnishing completely how astonishing it actually is in person, and this is irrespective of whether you are religious or not, as the architecture and design are enough to steal your words. The basilica, which isn't even finished, towers over the local area and includes two façades, one depicting the birth of Jesus, the other, his death. Every nook and cranny of the building is intentional and every single decision has a purpose and a significance.

When you book to go and see it, which honestly if you haven't done yet then I strongly urge that you do; I suggest doing one of the tower tours with the audio guide. The audio guide is a wonderful addition to this trip and it really helps you to understand Gaudí's inspiration, and it makes sure you don't miss out on the tinier details which you may miss otherwise. Follow the tour in order and you will gain insight into the inner workings of every rock type, every lighting choice, every colour etc. which Gaudí meticulously planned with an unmatched precision. The stain glass windows are my favourite part, as even the colours that were chosen have significance and the size of these windows and the light they allow in, paints the whole interior in a kaleidoscope of colour.

You get to pick which façade towers you would like to visit, and I have done both. My favourite is the passion façade, as it offers more in horizonal views, but the nativity façade was the first façade and incorporates all the finest aspects of the Gothic style. Either way, I doubt you will be disappointed and I really hope you love it as much as I do.

La Sagrada Familia is expected to be finished in 2025, to commemorate the centennial anniversary of the death of Gaudí, so keep the date booked, as the finished piece will truly be something to behold.

50. WHAT CAN BARCELONA TEACH YOU ABOUT YOURSELF?

This is a little bit off the topic of tourism, but it you have come out here alone and taken the time to get to know the people, you will find that they are very similar to English people, but with one surprising distinction, they are probably better at sarcasm than even us! I kid you not, most of my Spanish friends are my sassiest friends and can give as good as they take.

I have said that they can come across as impatient and abrupt, but underneath that, they are very caring people who really try to accommodate everyone and have a very generous nature. I am half Irish but look like I'm Scandinavian, so clearly not Spanish, yet I am always treated with a lot of respect, even if their words don't reflect their actions. Like I have said, taking a little time to learn a few key words, goes a long way, you will see that a few people's faces will light up when you do, as they see it as a kind of novelty, yet they will happily encourage you to keep trying.

Regardless of the type of trip you are going on, try and get some alone time for an hour or so, preferably outside, in nature or in the bustling city of this foreign country and just reflect. In an age where too many things separate us, I think it can be really satisfying to know that the rest of the world is composed of the same people, the same faces and the same personalities which you are likely accustomed to in your home town.

Wherever your trip takes you, I hope you enjoy Barcelona and live life like a native.

For Now, Hasta Luego.

Harrison Callaghan

TOP REASONS TO BOOK THIS TRIP

The Art: It is everywhere, it is unescapable, but when it is this pretty, why would you ever want to?

The Food: Never have I tasted a fish so good, and never has the smell of cooking made my mouth water as much.

The people: If you are staying here a while and happen to become friendly with some natives, cherish them, for they will be some of the fiercest friends you will ever have.

Harrison Callaghan

Bonus Book

50 THINGS TO KNOW ABOUT PACKING LIGHT FOR TRAVEL

Pack the Right Way Every Time

Author: Manidipa
Bhattacharyya

Harrison Callaghan

Edited by Melanie Howthorne

Introduction

*He who would travel happily
must travel light.*

-Antoine de Saint-Exupéry

Travel takes you to different places from seas and mountains to deserts and much more. In your travels you get to interact with different people and their cultures. You will, however, enjoy the sights and interact positively with these new people even more, if you are travelling light.

When you travel light your mind can be free from worry about your belongings. You do not have to spend precious vacation time waiting for your luggage to arrive after a long flight. There is be no chance of your bags going missing and the best part is that you need not pay a fee for checked baggage.

People who have mastered this art of packing light will root for you to take only one carry-on, wherever you go. However, many people can find it really hard to pack light. More so if you are travelling with children. Differentiating between "must have" and "just in case" items is the starting point. There will be ample shopping avenues at your destination which are just waiting to be explored.

Harrison Callaghan

This book will show you 'packing' in a new 'light' –
pun intended – and help you to embrace light
packing practices for all of your future travels.

Off to packing!

Dedication

I dedicate this book to all the travel buffs that I know,
who have given me great insights into the contents of
their backpacks.

About The Author

Manidipa Bhattacharyya is a creative writer and editor, with an education in English literature and Linguistics. After working in the IT industry for seven long years she decided to call it quits and follow her heart instead. Manidipa has been ghost writing, editing, proof reading and doing secondary research services for many story tellers and article writers for about three years. She stays in Kolkata, India with her husband and a busy two year old. In her own time Manidipa enjoys travelling, photography and writing flash fiction.

Manidipa believes in travelling light and never carries anything that she couldn't haul herself on a trip. However, travelling with her child changed the scenario. She seemed to carry the entire world with her for the baby on the first two trips. But good sense prevailed and she is again working her way to becoming a light traveler, this time with a kid.

The Right Travel Gear

1. Choose Your Travel Gear Carefully

While selecting your travel gear, pick items that are light weight, durable and most importantly, easy to carry. There are cases with wheels so you can drag them along – these are usually on the heavy side because of the trolley. Alternatively a backpack that you can carry comfortably on your back, or even a duffel bag that you can carry easily by hand or sling across your body are also great options. Whatever you choose, one thing to keep in mind is that the luggage itself should not weigh a ton, this will give you the flexibility to bring along one extra pair of shoes if you so desire.

2. Carry The Minimum Number Of Bags

Selecting light weight luggage is not everything. You need to restrict the number of bags you carry as well. One carry-on size bag is ideal for light travel. Most carriers allow one cabin baggage plus one purse, handbag or camera bag as long as it slides under the seat in front. So technically, you can carry two items of luggage without checking them in.

3. Pack One Extra Bag

Always pack one extra empty bag along with your essential items. This could be a very light weight duffel bag or even a sturdy tote bag which takes up minimal space. In the event that you end up buying a lot of souvenirs, you already have a handy bag to stuff all that into and do not have to spend time hunting for an appropriate bag.

I'm very strict with my packing and have everything in its right place. I never change a rule. I hardly use anything in the hotel room. I wheel my own wardrobe in and that's it.

Charlie Watts

Clothes & Accessories

4. Plan Ahead

Figure out in advance what you plan to do on your trip. That will help you to pick that one dress you need for the occasion. If you are going to attend a wedding then you have to carry formal wear. If not, you can ditch the gown for something lighter that will be comfortable during long walks or on the beach.

5. Wear That Jacket

Remember that wearing items will not add extra luggage for your air travel. So wear that bulky jacket that you plan to carry for your trip. This saves space and can also help keep you warm during the chilly flight.

6. Mix and Match

Carry clothes that can be interchangeably used to reinvent your look. Find one top that goes well with a couple of pairs of pants or skirts. Use tops, shirts and jackets wisely along with other accessories like a scarf or a stole to create a new look.

7. Choose Your Fabric Wisely

Stuffing clothes in cramped bags definitely takes its toll which results in wrinkles. It is best to carry wrinkle free, synthetic clothes or merino tops. This will eliminate the need for that small iron you usually bring along.

8. Ditch Clothes Pack Underwear

Pack more underwear and socks. These are the things that will give you a fresh feel even if you do not get a chance to wear fresh clothes. Moreover these are easy to wash and can be dried inside the hotel room itself.

9. Choose Dark Over Light

While picking your clothes choose dark coloured ones. They are easy to colour coordinate and can last longer before needing a wash. Accidental food spills and dirt from the road are less visible on darker clothes.

10. Wear Your Jeans

Take only one pair of Jeans with you, which you should wear on the flight. Remember to pick a pair that can be worn for sightseeing trips and is equally eloquent for dinner. You can add variety by adding light weight cargoes and chinos.

11. Carry Smart Accessories

The right accessory can give you a fresh look even with the same old dress. An intelligent neck-piece, a couple of bright scarves, stoles or a sarong can be used in a number of ways to add variety to your clothing. These light weight beauties can double up as a nursing cover, a light blanket, beach wear, a modesty cover for visiting places of worship, and also makes for an enthralling game of peek-a-boo.

12. Learn To Fold Your Garments

Seasoned travellers all swear by rolling their clothes for compact and wrinkle free packing. Bundle packing, where you roll the clothes around a central object as if tying it up, is also a popular method of compact and wrinkle free packing. Stacking folded clothes one on top of another is a big no-no as it makes creases extreme and they are difficult to get rid of without ironing.

13. Wash Your Dirty Laundry

One of the ways to avoid carrying loads of clothes is to wash the clothes you carry. At some places you might get to use the laundry services or a Laundromat but if you are in a pinch, best solution is to wash them yourself. If that is the plan then carrying quick drying clothes is highly recommended, which most often also happen to be the wrinkle free variety.

14. Leave Those Towels Behind

Regular towels take up a lot of space, are heavy and take ages to dry out. If you are staying at hotels they will provide you with towels anyway. If you are travelling to a remote place, where the availability of towels look doubtful, carry a light weight travel towel of viscose material to do the job.

15. Use A Compression Bag

Compression bags are getting lots of recommendation now days from regular travellers. These are useful for saving space in your luggage when you have to pack bulky dresses. While packing for the return trip, get help from the hotel staff to arrange a vacuum cleaner.

Footwear

16. Put On Your Hiking Boots

If you have plans to go hiking or trekking during your trip, you will need those bulky hiking boots. The best way to carry them is to wear them on flight to save space and luggage weight. You can remove the boots once inside and be comfortable in your socks.

17. Picking The Right Shoes

Shoes are often the bulkiest items, along with being the dainty if you are a female. They need care and take up a lot of space in your luggage. It is advisable therefore to pick shoes very carefully. If you plan to do a lot of walking and site seeing, then wearing a pair of comfortable walking shoes are a must. For more formal occasions you can carry durable, light weight flats which will not take up much space.

18. Stuff Shoes

If you happen to pack a pair of shoes, ensure you utilize their hollow insides. Tuck small items like rolled up socks or belts to save space. They will also be easy to find.

Toiletries
19. Stashing Toiletries

Carry only absolute necessities. Airline rules dictate that for one carry-on bag, liquids and gels must be in 3.4 ounce (100ml) bottles or less, and must be packed in a one quart zip-lock bag. If you are planning to stay in a hotel, the basic things will be provided for you. It's best is to buy the rest from the local market at your destination.

20. Take Along Tampons

Tampons are a hard to find item in a lot of countries.
Figure out how many you need and pack accordingly.
For longer stays you can buy them online and have
them delivered to where you are staying.

21. Get Pampered Before You Travel

Some avid travellers suggest getting a pedicure and
manicure just the day before travelling. This not only
gives you a well kept look, you also save the trouble
of packing nail polish. Remember, every little bit of
weight reduced adds up.

Electronics
22. Lugging Along Electronics

Electronics have a large role to play in our lives
today. Most of us cannot imagine our lives away from
our phones, laptops or tablets. However while
travelling, one must consider the amount of weight
these electronics add to our luggage. Thankfully
smart phones come along with all the essentials tools
like a camera, email access, picture editing tools and
more. They are smart to the point of eliminating the
need to carry multiple gadgets. Choose a smart phone

that suits all your requirements and travel with the world in your palms or pocket.

23. Reduce the Number of Chargers

If you do travel with multiple electronic devices, you will have to bear the additional burden of carrying all their chargers too. Check if a single charger can be used for multiple devices. You might also consider investing in a pocket charger. These small devices support multiple devices while keeping you charged on the go.

24. Travel Friendly Apps

Along with smart phones come numerous apps, which are immensely helpful in our travels. You name it and you have an app for it at hand – take pictures, sharing with friends and family, torch to light dark roads, maps, checking flight/train times, find hotels and many other things. Use these smart alternatives to traditional items like books to eliminate weight and save space.

I get ideas about what's essential when packing my suitcase.

-Diane von Furstenberg

Travelling With Kids

25. Bring Along the Stroller

Kids might enjoy walking for a while but they soon tire out and a stroller is the just the right thing for them to rest in while you continue your tour. Strollers also double duty as a luggage carrier and shopping bag holder. Remember to pick a light weight, easy to handle brand of stroller. Better yet, find out in advance if you can rent a stroller at your destination.

26. Bring Only Enough Diapers for Your Trip

Diapers take up a lot of space and add to the weight of your luggage. Therefore it is advisable to carry just enough diapers to last through the trip and a few for afterwards, till you buy fresh stock at your destination. Unless of course you are travelling to a really remote area, in which case you have no choice but to carry the load. Otherwise diapers are something you will find pretty easily.

27. Take Only A Couple Of Toys

Children are easily attracted by new things in their environment. While travelling they will find numerous 'new' objects to scrutinize and play with. Packing just one favorite toy is enough, or if there is no favorite toy leave out all of them in favor of stories or imaginary games.

28. Carry Kid Friendly Snacks

Create a small snack counter in your bag to store away quick bites for those sudden hunger pangs. Depending on the child's age this could include chocolates, raisins, dry fruits, granola bars or biscuits. Also keep a bottle of water handy for your little one. These things do not add much weight and can be adjusted in a handbag or knapsack.

29. Games to Carry

Create some travel specific, imaginary games if you have slightly grown up children, like spot the attractions. Keep a coloring book and colors handy for in-flight or hotel time. Apps on your smart phone can keep the children engaged with cartoons and story books. Older children are often entertained by games available on phones or tablets. This cuts the weight of luggage down while keeping the kids entertained.

30. Let the Kids Carry Their Load

A good thing is to start early sharing of responsibilities. Let your child pick a bag of his or her choice and pack it themselves. Keep tabs on what they are stuffing in their bags by asking if they will be using that item on the trip. It could start out being just an entertainment bag initially but with growing years they will learn to sort the useful from the superfluous. Children as little as four can maneuver a small trolley suitcase like a pro- their experience in pull along toys credit. If you are worried that you may be pulling it for them, you may want to start with a backpack.

31. Decide on Location for Children to Sleep

While on a trip you might not always get a crib at your destination, and carrying one will make life all the more difficult. Instead call ahead to see if there are any cribs or roll out beds for children. You may even put blankets on the floor. Weave them a story about camping and they will gladly sleep without any trouble.

32. Get Baby Products Delivered At Your Destination

If you are absolutely paranoid about not getting your favourite variety of diaper or brand of baby food, check out online stores like amazon.com for services in your destination city. You can buy things online ahead of your travel and get them delivered to your hotel upon arrival.

33. Feeding Needs Of Your Infants

If you are travelling with a breastfed infant, you save the trouble of carrying bottles and bottle sanitization kits. For special food, or medications, you may need to call ahead to make sure you have a refrigerator where you are staying.

34. Feeding Needs of Your Toddler

With the progression from infancy to toddler, their dietary requirements too evolve. You will have to pack some snacks for travelling time. Fresh fruits and vegetables can be purchased at your destination. Most of the cities you travel to in whichever part of the world, will have baby food products and formulas, available at the local drug-store or the supermarket.

35. Picking Clothes for Your Baby

Contrary to popular belief, babies can do without many changes of clothes. At the most pack 2 outfits per day. Pack mix and match type clothes for your little one as well. Pick things which are comfortable to wear and quick to dry.

36. Selecting Shoes for Your Baby

Like outfits, kids can make do with two pairs of comfortable shoes. If you can get some water resistant shoes it will be best. To expedite drying wet shoes, you can stuff newspaper in them then wrap them with newspaper and leave them to dry overnight.

37. Keep One Change of Clothes Handy

Travelling with kids can be tricky. Keep a change of clothes for the kids and mum handy in your purse or tote bag. This takes a bit of space in your hand luggage but comes extremely handy in case there are any accidents or spills.

38. Leave Behind Baby Accessories

Baby accessories like their bed, bath tub, car seat, crib etc. should be left at home. Many hotels provide a crib on request, while car seats can be borrowed from friends or rented. Babies can be given a bath in the hotel sink or even in the adult bath tub with a little bit of water. If you bring a few bath toys, they can be used in the bath, pool, and out of water. They can also be sanitized easily in the sink.

39. Carry a Small Load Of Plastic Bags

With children around there are chances of a number of soiled clothes and diapers. These plastic bags help to sort the dirt from the clean inside your big bag. These are very light weight and come in handy to other carry stuff as well at times.

Pack with a Purpose

40. Packing for Business Trips

One neutral-colored suit should suffice. It can be paired with different shirts, ties and accessories for different occasions. One pair of black suit pants could be worn with a matching jacket for the office or with a snazzy top for dinner.

41. Packing for A Cruise

Most cruises have formal dinners, and that formal dress usually takes up a lot of space. However you might find a tuxedo to rent. For women, a short black dress with multiple accessory options will do the trick.

42. Packing for A Long Trip Over Different Climates

The secret packing mantra for travel over multiple climates is layering. Layering traps air around your body creating insulation against the cold. The same light t-shirt that is comfortable in a warmer climate can be the innermost layer in a colder climate.

Reduce Some More Weight

43. Leave Precious Things At Home

Things that you would hate to lose or get damaged leave them at home. Precious jewelry, expensive gadgets or dresses, could be anything. You will not require these on your trip. Leave them at home and spare the load on your mind.

44. Send Souvenirs by Mail

If you have spent all your money on purchasing souvenirs, carrying them back in the same bag that you brought along would be difficult. Either pack everything in another bag and check it in the airport or get everything shipped to your home. Use an international carrier for a secure transit, but this could be more expensive than the checking fees at the airport.

45. Avoid Carrying Books

Books equal to weight. There are many reading apps which you can download on your smart phone or tab. Plus there are gadgets like Kindle and Nook that are thinner and lighter alternatives to your regular book.

Check, Get, Set, Check Again

46. Strategize Before Packing

Create a travel list and prepare all that you think you need to carry along. Keep everything on your bed or floor before packing and then think through once again – do I really need that? Any item that meets this question can be avoided. Remove whatever you don't really need and pack the rest.

47. Test Your Luggage

Once you have fully packed for the trip take a test trip with your luggage. Take your bags and go to town for window shopping for an hour. If you enjoy your hour long trip it is good to go, if not, go home and reduce the load some more. Repeat this test till you hit the right weight.

48. Add a Roll Of Duct Tape

You might wonder why, when this book has been talking about reducing stuff, we're suddenly asking you to pack something totally unusual. This is because when you have limited supplies, duct tape is immensely helpful for small repairs – a broken bag, leaking zip-lock bag, broken sunglasses, you name it and duct tape can fix it, temporarily.

49. List of Essential Items

Even though the emphasis is on packing light, there are things which have to be carried for any trip. Here is our list of essentials:

- Passport/Visa or any other ID

- Any other paper work that might be required on a trip like permits, hotel reservation confirmations etc.

- Medicines – all your prescription medicines and emergency kit, especially if you are travelling with children

- Medical or vaccination records

- Money in foreign currency if travelling to a different country

- Tickets- Email or Message them to your phone

50. Make the Most of Your Trip

Wherever you are going, whatever you hope to do we encourage you to embrace it whole-heartedly. Take in the scenery, the culture and above all, enjoy your time away from home.

On a long journey even a straw weighs heavy.

-Spanish Proverb

Packing and Planning Tips

A Week before Leaving

- Arrange for someone to take care of pets and water plants

- •Stop mail and newspaper

- Notify Credit Card companies where you are going.

- Change your thermostat settings

- Car inspected, oil is changed, and tires have the correct pressure.

- Passports and id is up to date.

- Pay bills.

- Copy important items and download travel Apps.

- Start collecting small bills for tips

Right Before Leaving

- Clean out refrigerator.

- Empty garbage cans.

- Lock windows.

- Make sure you have the right ID with you.

- Bring cash for tips.

- Remember travel documents.

- Lock door behind you.

- Remember wallet.

- Unplug items in house and pack chargers.

115

Harrison Callaghan

Read other
Greater Than a Tourist
Books

Greater Than a Tourist San Miguel de Allende Guanajuato Mexico:
50 Travel Tips from a Local by Tom Peterson

Greater Than a Tourist – Lake George Area New York USA:
50 Travel Tips from a Local by Janine Hirschklau

Greater Than a Tourist – Monterey California United States:
50 Travel Tips from a Local by Katie Begley

Greater Than a Tourist – Chanai Crete Greece:
50 Travel Tips from a Local by Dimitra Papagrigoraki

Greater Than a Tourist – The Garden Route Western Cape Province
South Africa:
50 Travel Tips from a Local by Li-Anne McGregor van Aardt

Greater Than a Tourist – Sevilla Andalusia Spain:
50 Travel Tips from a Local by Gabi Gazon

Greater Than a Tourist – Kota Bharu Kelantan Malaysia:
50 Travel Tips from a Local by Aditi Shukla

Children's Book: Charlie the Cavalier Travels the World by Lisa
Rusczyk

Harrison Callaghan

> TOURIST

Visit Greater Than a Tourist for Free Travel Tips
http://GreaterThanATourist.com

Sign up for the Greater Than a Tourist Newsletter for
discount days, new books, and travel information:
http://eepurl.com/cxspyf

Follow us on Facebook for tips, images, and ideas:
https://www.facebook.com/GreaterThanATourist

Follow us on Pinterest for travel tips and ideas:
http://pinterest.com/GreaterThanATourist

Follow us on Instagram for beautiful travel images:
http://Instagram.com/GreaterThanATourist

Harrison Callaghan

> TOURIST

Please leave your honest review of this book on Amazon and Goodreads. Please send your feedback to GreaterThanaTourist@gmail.com as we continue to improve the series. Thank you. We appreciate your positive and constructive feedback. Thank you.

Harrison Callaghan

NOTES

Printed in Great Britain
by Amazon